Copyright @ 2018 Nutrition Associates, LLC

All rights reserved. No part of this book may be reproduced, transmitted, or stored in an information retrieval system in any form or by any means, graphic, electronic, or mechanical, including photography, taping, and recording without prior written permission from the author.

First U.S. edition 2018

ISBN-13: 978-0692118030 (Custom Universal)

ISBN-10: 0692118039

Illustrations were done by Rob Peters in pen and ink on Bristol paper and digitally painted in Photoshop.

All matters regarding weight management and health require medical supervision. The author is not engaged in rendering professional/medical/health advice or services to children and their families or caregivers. The ideas, procedures, and suggestions contained in this book are not intended as substitutes for consulting with your medical/health care provider. The author shall not be liable or responsible for any loss or damage allegedly arising from information or suggestions in this book. The author does not assume any responsibility for errors or for changes that occur after publication. The author does not have any control over and does not assume any responsibility for author or third-party websites or their content.

To contact Dr. Roni Roth Beshears for a speaking engagement and presentation, email her at roni.nutritionassociates@gmail.com.

For additional information, please visit the Roni Children's Book Series website at www.ronichildrenseries.com.

For MVB
 —RRB

FOREWORD

Roni Discovers Mindfulness is the fourth book in a series on weight management and wellness for school-age children and their families. The book incorporates mindfulness strategies to help children become aware of the eating process and internal body signals that guide food regulation. *"Eight Mindful Eating and Lifestyle Tips for Kids"* are included to help children begin the journey toward a more mindful way of living.

Other books in the Roni Children's Book Series:

Please Don't Call Me Chubby Roni! is a story about the harm that name-calling causes in a school setting for a young girl. The actions taken by the main character, Roni, and her teacher raise awareness about weight-based name-calling in the classroom. The book serves to open communication with children, parents, and teachers about negative body-size talk and the impact it can have on children.

Roni Goes to Camp is a story about a summer camp experience for Roni, a young girl who is overweight and is attending camp for the first time. Her problems at camp and their resolution with the help of supportive staff and counselors offer children, especially young girls like Roni, valuable lessons in self-awareness and self-management.

Roni Takes Action is a call-to-action story about a young girl, Roni, who is teased by schoolmates and embarrassed by her unsatisfactory school physical fitness report. With the help of a dietitian, Roni and her family take action to improve their food plan and health. The story offers simple and practical changes to guide children who are overweight, as well as their families, to achieve a balanced and healthy lifestyle.

The *Roni Children's Book Series* (www.ronichildrenseries.com) is an educational and engaging teaching tool on weight management and wellness for school-age children and their families. Roni is a strong and confident young girl who wants to empower children to have a positive self-image and embrace a healthy lifestyle.

Places for book distribution are homes, libraries, schools, community centers, and medical practices. The series supports the establishment of non-threatening and wholesome environments to help children grow, learn, and accomplish their dreams.

Thanks to:

Adrienne Forman, MS, RDN, a child weight-management specialist with the MEND (www.healthyweightpartnership.org) program.

Deborah Markenson, MS

Karen Stephens, MS, RD, CSP, LD

Karen Josiah, MS, RD, LD

Children's Mercy Hospital, Kansas City, Missouri

One day after school, I went over to my best friend Rosa's house to do homework.

"Hi, Manny," I said to Rosa's older brother. "What are you playing?"

Manny didn't answer me.

"What's wrong, Manny?" I asked.

He slowly turned his head. "I'm not going to be a starter on the school soccer team. I'm just one of the substitute players."

Rosa and I looked at each other with surprise.

"Wow, I can't believe it," Rosa told him. "You're great at soccer."

"The coach told me I wasn't trying my best. He said I wasn't ready when the ball came my way." Then Manny turned back to his video game.

"You're feeling bad, Manny, I can tell," Rosa said.

"Why don't you ask the coach what you can do to improve your game? He likes you. I know he'll help."

"Don't give up, Manny," I said.

The next morning at school, Mrs. Deluca, told the class, "We have a special guest coming later this morning."

"Mrs. Smith, the food service dietitian or 'lunch lady' as you call her, will lead the class in a demonstration of mindful eating."

Rosa turned around in her seat. "Roni, what's mindful eating?"

"I have no clue," I said.

At midmorning, Mrs. Smith came into the classroom and said, "Good morning, everyone."

"As you know, I work in the lunchroom, planning the school meals and hanging nutrition information posters all over the cafeteria."

"Today, we are going on a journey of self-discovery."

"Every day most people eat three meals – breakfast, lunch, and dinner," she said.

"I know you eat lunch because I see you in the lunchroom."

"When you eat," she asked, "do you give your full attention to eating or do you gobble your food down quickly?"

Most of us looked puzzled. What does she mean?

"Let me explain," Mrs. Smith continued.

"Raise your hand if you eat in front of television."

Almost everyone raised a hand.

"Is your attention on eating food or watching TV? It's difficult to do both at the same time," she said.

"Let me show you what I mean by paying attention to what you eat."

Mrs. Smith gave each student a paper plate and napkin. Then she put two raisins on every plate.

"Pick up one raisin," she told us. "Put the raisin in your mouth and eat it the way you usually do."

She waited a couple of minutes.

"Now, pick up the second raisin," she said. "But don't eat it yet!"

"Look at the shape of the raisin, the surface, and the color. Notice how it feels between your fingers."

Moving around the classroom, Mrs. Smith asked a bunch of questions.

"Is the raisin big or small?"

"Golden brown or dark brown?"

"Soft or hard?"

"Wrinkly or smooth?"

"Now, bring the raisin up to your nose," she said. "What does it smell like?"

"Sweet," someone replied.

Another student disagreed. "The raisin has no smell."

"Both students are correct," Mrs. Smith said. "That may sound surprising. But each person appreciates the qualities of food differently."

Finally, it was time to eat the second raisin!

"Hold on!" Mrs. Smith said immediately. "Let's eat this raisin slowly, v-e-r-y slowly."

Mrs. Smith told us to place the raisin on our tongue.

"Feel the size and texture of the raisin as you move it around in your mouth. Gradually the raisin softens as you chew it," she explained.

"That's the beginning of digestion, which is the body's process of breaking down food for energy and health."

A student spoke up. "I usually eat raisins by the handful."

Mrs. Smith nodded. "Lots of people do," she said. "But eating a bunch of raisins really fast can lead you to miss out on the total eating experience."

"Try to slow down and taste your food."

Placing her hand on her stomach, Mrs. Smith asked, "Does your stomach feel full, satisfied, or empty?"

She drew a line on the board with the number 10 (feeling very full or stuffed) at one end, the number 5 in the middle (feeling satisfied), and the number 1 at the other end (feeling very hungry or empty).

"Now, write down the number that rates how your stomach feels right now," she told us. "After lunch, I will ask you to score your hunger-fullness level again."

On the way to lunch, Norma and I talked about class. "I gave myself a 3 because I had breakfast," I said.

Norma looked down at the floor. "Roni, I never eat breakfast before school," she said. "My mom leaves for work early and there's not much food at home."

I was speechless. I didn't know what to say to Norma.

"Hey, Norma," I said as we went into the cafeteria, "let's sit together."

Rosa joined us at our table.

"I'm starving. I'm on empty," she said as she sat down and began eating quickly. "I left home without breakfast today. I was late for school."

"Slow down," I said to Rosa. "Remember, we're eating mindfully."

Norma, Rosa, and I lifted up our forks together.
"Let's see who can chew for the longest time," I said.
We took turns counting bites after each mouthful of food.
It seemed silly, but it sure made us slow down.

When we finished lunch, I said, "Let's have breakfast at school tomorrow morning."

"Eating school breakfast would be good for me," Rosa said. "I have a bad habit of being late and missing breakfast at home."

Norma nodded. "I would feel better having breakfast with both of you. I don't like to eat breakfast alone in the cafeteria."

"It's a deal," I said.

Mrs. Smith was waiting for us in our classroom.

"Welcome back, students," she said. "Please write down the number that rates your hunger-fullness level now."

After a moment, she asked us, "How many of you chose 10, feeling very full or stuffed?"

No one raised a hand.

"What about 5?"

Hands went up. Most of the class felt satisfied after their lunch.

Mrs. Smith told us, "It's helpful to be aware of your stomach signals before and after eating. Eat when you are hungry, and eat just enough to feel satisfied, not stuffed."

Then Mrs. Smith asked, "Were any of you able to slow down and really enjoy your lunch today?"

Rosa, Norma, and I raised our hands and nodded our heads yes.

One boy said, "Lunch was good, but the lunchroom was so noisy I could hardly hear myself talk."

Mrs. Smith said, "Yes, loud noise can distract us or interrupt our focus on eating."

"Other distractions are watching television, reading a book, or texting on a smartphone at mealtime. If you can avoid distractions when you're eating, you're likely to enjoy your meals more."

As Mrs. Smith was leaving the room, she said, "Have a great day and practice mindfulness."

After school, I went to Rosa's house for dinner.

"Come in, Roni," Rosa's mom said as she gave me a hug.

On the kitchen table was lots of foods -- vegetable salad, beans and rice, chicken enchiladas, sliced mangoes, and milk.

I always love eating dinner with Rosa's family.

"Like your family, Roni, we're trying to eat healthy," said Mrs. Gonzales.

"Eating together as a family and enjoying our favorite foods is important to us."

When everyone was sitting at the table, Rosa said, "In school today, the lunch lady, Mrs. Smith, taught us about mindful eating."

"What's that?" Manny asked with a chuckle.

"Don't laugh, Manny," I said. "Mindful eating is about paying attention to our body and eating with awareness."

Suddenly, Rosa got up from the table, walked over to the television, and turned it off.

"Television is a distraction when you're eating," she announced.

I thought, Mrs. Smith would be proud of Rosa.

"Let's practice mindful eating," Rosa said to everyone.

"Now, place a forkful of food in your mouth. Chew your food and silently count to ten before swallowing."

"Wow, I never ate so slowly," Manny said when we had all finished. "I usually race through dinner and rush back to the computer."

"Manny," Rosa said, "eating slowly helps us tune in to our stomach signals and realize when we've had enough to eat."

Mrs. Gonzales looked at her husband and children. "That means I should ask if you want a second helping of food before I give you any more."

As we began clearing the table, Mr. Gonzales said, "I think your class today was very valuable. Respecting your body and bringing your full awareness to eating and other activities is an important lesson."

He looked at his son. "Manny," he said, "I think you should get back on the soccer field and bring your full attention to the game. Don't get distracted, just focus on the ball. I know you will make the starting soccer team."

Manny stood up, grabbed his soccer ball, and ran to the park across the street to practice before it got dark.

Later that week, I talked with Mrs. Deluca after school.

"A friend in class does not have food at home for breakfast," I told her. "But she's afraid kids will tease her if she eats breakfast in the cafeteria."

Mrs. Deluca nodded. "I realize some students don't have enough food to eat at home. It's a real problem. Kids need breakfast to be successful in school," she said.

"Mom and I would like to talk with you about doing 'breakfast-in-the-classroom,'" I said.

Mrs. Deluca smiled at me. "Great idea! Let's meet tomorrow before school starts. And Roni, it's wonderful that you have such kind and caring feelings for others."

Rosa was waiting for me. When we walked outside, we saw Manny on the soccer field.

He looked fierce and he was charged-up and ready to go.

While we watched, Manny kicked the soccer ball hard and scored a goal for his team.

Rosa and I jumped up and down with excitement.

I said to Rosa, "Success doesn't always happen overnight, but it sure helps to be mindful."

Afterword

Raising healthy children is a goal for parents, caregivers, and society. Good food, proper nutrition, and a healthy lifestyle are key ingredients for positive growth, development, and learning. Mindfulness teaches kids to trust themselves, their bodies, and their natural instincts.

When we are mindful, experts say, we bring our total being and whole heart to all our activities. Through mindfulness training, children have the opportunity to learn and apply valuable skills for personal inquiry and insight.

Mindfulness practices are combined in this book as a way to introduce students to these concepts. Relatable characters and mindfulness learning activities in school and at home are woven into a story to demonstrate the value of these strategies for children. The mindfulness education movement is now growing and expanding all over the country. This book can be used as a teaching tool and educational resource to help children discover how to eat and live in a more mindful way.

Let's give kids a mindfulness chance!

Eight Mindful Eating and Lifestyle Tips For Kids

1. Honor your individuality and the unique sensory qualities of food.
2. Slow down, enjoy your food, and give your full attention to eating.
3. Become aware of your internal stomach signals and rate your hunger-fullness level before and after you eat.
4. Enjoy the company of family and friends at meals.
5. Avoid "distractors" while eating, such as watching television, reading a book, or texting on a smartphone.
6. Show kindness and caring for others, especially those who are less fortunate and who may be food-insecure, by sharing food and spending mealtimes together.
7. Bring your full awareness to everything you do, including sports and other types of physical activity. It's worth the effort.
8. Success doesn't happen overnight. Living mindfully is a lifelong journey.

Recommended Online Resources

American Federation of Teachers
   www.aft.org/childrens-health/nutrition/breakfast-in-the-classroom

Daniel Rechtschaffen, MFT, founding director of **Mindful Education** and author of *The Mindful Education Workbook: Lessons for Teaching Mindfulness to Students*
                              www.danielrechtschaffen.com

Evelyn Tribole, MS, RD, and Elyse Resch, MS, RD, intuitive eating specialists and authors of *Intuitive Eating: A Revolutionary Program That Works*
                              www.intuitiveeating.org

International Food Information Council Foundation
                   www.foodinsight.org/mindful-intuitive-eating-
                              differences-eating-pattern

Linda Lantieri, MA, founding member and senior program advisor for CASEL (Collaborative for Academic, Social, and Emotional Learning), Adjunct Assistant Professor, Columbia University, Teachers College and author of *Building Emotional Intelligence*
                              www.lindalantieri.org

About the Author

As an advanced-level registered dietitian, nutritionist, and certified health and wellness coach, **Dr. Roni Roth Beshears** has worked at the local, state, and federal levels with food and nutrition programs and services. As a community volunteer and advocate, she has devoted time and energy to serving the needs of vulnerable women, children, and families. Dr. Roth Beshears established Nutrition Associates LLC and is the creator and author of the Roni Children's Book Series. She is a graduate of Syracuse University (BS) and Columbia University, Teachers College (EdD).

www.ingramcontent.com/pod-product-compliance
Lightning Source LLC
LaVergne TN
LVHW071029070426
835507LV00002B/75